Oliver and the Anxiety Monster

by Roger Schrader

For my family, whose love and support make every day brighter.

And to all the brave kids facing their own Worry Wumpuses - you are stronger than you know.

Table of Contents

1. Introduction
2. The Best Summer Ever
3. Back to School Worries
4. Struggling but Not Alone
5. Meeting Worry Wumpus
6. Learning to Cope
7. The Power of Sharing
8. More Coping Methods
9. First Day of School
10. A New Routine
11. Embracing Worry Wumpus
12. Conclusion
13. Author's Note

Introduction

Once upon a time, in a small friendly town surrounded by rolling hills and lush forests, lived a young boy named Oliver. He was bright, curious, and cheery, with a great love for adventures and making new friends. His contagious laugh would light up faces around him, and in his chest lay a heart filled with dreams and wonders.

Oliver's family resided in a small cozy house at the edge of the town, next to the beautiful forest. The smell from the morning dew, the singing of the birds, and the rising of the sun over the hills were among his favorite things to view each morning.

Chapter 1. The Best Summer Ever

Oliver was full of energy, and imagination and adventure. He made a treehouse on the top of the tallest tree standing in the forest near his house. The treehouse became his special place for fun and adventure. From there, he could see the entire town and way beyond. A lot of hours went by while he was in his treehouse, pretending to be a pirate searching for his treasure, an astronaut seeking different planets, or a brave knight protecting his castle.

Oliver, Jake, and Mia made up a trio of friends who spent summer days having great adventures in the woods. Joking Jake would never stop joking and sometimes not laughing either. Mia was the bravest, always leading through the thickest parts of the woods. Every day was a discovery, and by evening, Oliver always had stories to tell when he came home.

Oliver's family was very close. His parents adored him and encouraged his love for exploration of the world and adventures. They often would go with him to explore nature, science, and the environment. His mom was an artist and used to paint scenes he returned with from his adventures. His father, who was a writer, would create stories about their times together.

They had the weekly family night where they played games, watched movies, or went on picnics in the forest. Besides Oliver, he also had a little sister, Lily, whom he adored and took with him often. He sometimes brought her into the forest on one of his goose chases, parading through it, showing her every wondrous detail. Lily adored Oliver greatly, and the two were very close friends.

This summer had been the best one yet. Oliver had built the grandest treehouse with his dad, complete with a wood ladder, a lookout post, and a small shelf for his favorite books and treasures. He had explored deeper into the woods than ever, discovering a hidden pond where they would catch frogs and watch dragonflies dance over the water.

Oliver had also made new friends. He met Sam and Emma at the local summer camp. Sam loved to invent new games, while Emma had a talent for finding the best hiding spots. Together, they quickly became part of his adventure crew. They had water balloon fights, camped out under the stars, and even put on a play for their families, showcasing their wild imaginations.

Oliver was naturally confident and happy. He enjoyed school, had good grades, and was well-liked by his classmates. His teachers often praised his enthusiasm and willingness to help others. He loved learning new things and was always eager to participate in class activities.

His friends admired him for his bravery and creativity. They knew they could always count on Oliver for a fun time and exciting adventures. He was the glue that held his group of friends together, always coming up with new games to play and stories to tell.

As summer drew to a close, Oliver felt a mix of excitement and sadness. He loved school and was looking forward to seeing his friends again, but he also didn't want the summer adventures to end. He sat in his favorite treehouse, looking out at the sunset, thinking about all the fun he had. Just then, his parents called him inside.

"Oliver, it is time we prepare for the upcoming school year!" his mom said. "You are going to be a third grader soon!"

As soon as Oliver heard the word "school," he felt a strange knot in his stomach. His heart started to race, and his palms got sweaty. He did not understand why he felt this way. School had always been okay, but this year felt different.

Chapter 2: Back to School Worries

Oliver tried to ignore the feeling, but it followed him everywhere. When he was playing with his toys, watching TV, or even eating his favorite ice cream, the nervousness would not go away. He found himself unable to focus on his favorite activities, feeling a constant sense of unease.

Oliver's friend, Jake, noticed that he wasn't as cheerful as usual. "Are you okay, Oliver?" Jake asked.

"I am not sure," Oliver replied. "I feel strange and nervous about school starting."

Later, Oliver called his friend Max, who would be in his class. They talked about the upcoming school year, and while Max seemed excited, Oliver's nervousness grew. "Do not worry, Oliver," Max said. "Our new teacher is supposed to be nice, and we can sit together at lunch!"

After the call, Oliver had many questions for his parents. "What if I forget something important? What if I do not understand the new subjects? How will I make new friends?" His parents listened patiently and reassured him. "It is normal to feel this way, Oliver," his mom said. "Just take it one day at a time. You will do great."

That night, Oliver lay in bed, unable to fall asleep. Thoughts about school swirled in his mind. He imagined different scenarios, both good and bad, and wondered how he would handle them. He remembered his parent's advice and took a few deep breaths, trying to calm himself. Eventually, he drifted off, hoping for the best.

Chapter 3: Struggling but not Alone

Over the next few days, Oliver's behavior continued to change. He lost interest in his favorite activities, like playing outside, and building with his Legos, instead spending more time alone in his room. He avoided talking about school and pretended everything was fine. But the nervousness grew stronger, and he felt overwhelmed by a sense of dread.

Oliver's parents noticed he was quieter than usual and seemed unhappy. "Is everything okay, Oliver?" his dad asked one evening.

"Yes, everything is fine," Oliver replied quickly, not wanting to worry them. He did not know how to explain his feelings or that his parents could help him.

That night, Oliver had a dream. He was standing in a huge school hallway, surrounded by unfamiliar faces. He tried to find his classroom, but the hallways twisted and turned like a maze. His heart pounded, and he felt lost and alone. Suddenly, he woke up, his sheets tangled around him. He lay in the dark, trying to shake off the feeling of being trapped.

The next day, Oliver sat at his desk in his room with a blank piece of paper in front of him. He picked up a crayon and started drawing, hoping it would help distract him. He drew a picture of himself at school, surrounded by friends. But the picture did not match how he felt inside. He crumpled it up and tossed it aside, feeling frustrated.

Oliver's grandmother called that afternoon. She had a way of making him feel better, even when he was sad. "Hi, Oliver! How are you doing, my sweet boy?" she asked.

"I am okay," Oliver said, his voice barely a whisper.

"Just okay? That does not sound like my cheerful Oliver," she said gently. "Is something bothering you?"

Oliver hesitated, then blurted out, "I am scared about school starting."

"Oh, Oliver, it is normal to feel that way," his grandma said. "When I was your age, I felt the same way sometimes. Do you want to talk about it?"

Oliver took a deep breath and decided to share his feelings. "I do not know why, but I just feel so nervous about going back to school. What if I forget everything I learned last year? What if the other kids do not like me?"

His grandma listened carefully, her voice soothing and understanding. "I remember feeling the same way before a new school year," she said. "One thing that helped me was to talk about my worries. Sometimes, just saying them out loud makes them less scary."

"Really?" Oliver asked, feeling a bit relieved that someone understood.

"Yes, really," his grandma replied. "And you know what else helped? Making a plan. Let us think of some things you can do if you start to feel nervous."

Oliver nodded, feeling hopeful. "Like what?" he asked.

"Well," his grandma began, "how about we practice some deep breathing? When you start to feel anxious, take a few deep breaths. In through your nose, out through your mouth. Try it with me."

Oliver took a deep breath in, then slowly let it out. He did it a few more times, feeling a bit calmer with each breath.

"That feels nice," he admitted.

"Good," his grandma said. "Another thing you can do is think about something that makes you happy. Maybe a fun memory from the summer, or something you are looking forward to."

Oliver thought about the fun day he had at the beach with his family, building sandcastles and playing in the waves. The memory made him smile.

"And remember," his grandma continued, "you do not have to go through this alone. Your parents, your friends, and even your teachers are there to help you. You can always talk to them if you need to."

Oliver felt a warmth in his heart, knowing he had support. "Thanks, Grandma. I feel a little better now."

"Anytime, sweetheart," his grandma replied. "And if you ever need to talk, you can call me. I am always here for you."

That evening, as Oliver lay in bed, he felt a little more prepared for the days ahead. He still felt nervous, but he also felt a bit stronger. Maybe, just maybe, he could handle this after all.

Chapter 4: Meeting Worry Wumpus

One morning, after a restless night, Oliver woke up to find a small, fluffy creature sitting at the foot of his bed. It had big, round eyes and a worried expression.

"Who are you?" Oliver asked, sitting up quickly.

"I am Worry Wumpus," the creature said softly. "I am here because you're feeling anxious about school."

Oliver was surprised. "Anxious? Is that why I feel so nervous all the time?"

Worry Wumpus nodded. "Yes, Oliver. Anxiety is when you feel worried or scared about things that might happen. But don't worry, I am here to help you understand and cope with it."

Worry Wumpus shifted closer, his gentle eyes meeting Oliver's. "You see, Oliver, I am a reflection of your worries. Whenever you start to feel anxious, I appear."

Oliver looked puzzled. "So, you show up whenever I am worried?"

Worry Wumpus gave a small, comforting smile. "Because I am feeling what you are feeling. When you are anxious, I am too. It is like We are in this together."

Worry Wumpus continued, "My job isn't to make you feel worse. I am here to help you recognize your feelings. When you see me, it means you are worried about something, and that is okay."

Oliver sighed, feeling a bit more at ease. "So, you are not here to scare me?"

"Not at all," Worry Wumpus reassured him. "I am here to help you understand your anxiety. Sometimes just knowing that it is okay to feel this way can make a big difference."

Oliver nodded, thinking about his classmates. "So, other kids feel like this too?"

"Yes," Worry Wumpus said. "It is something everyone goes through at different times. It is a part of what makes us human."

Oliver decided to share more about his worries. "I have been feeling scared about going back to school. What if I cannot remember what I learned? What if the other kids don't like me?"

Worry Wumpus listened carefully. "Those are real concerns, Oliver. And it is brave of you to talk about them. By recognizing your worries, you are already taking the first step towards feeling better."

Oliver felt a small spark of hope. "I never thought about it that way."

"Whenever you see me, know that it is a sign you are dealing with something important," Worry Wumpus explained. "It is a reminder that you are not alone and that you have the strength to face your worries."

Oliver looked at Worry Wumpus with a new sense of understanding. "So, you are here to help me understand my feelings?"

"Exactly," Worry Wumpus replied. "And remember, your family and friends are here to support you too. You do not have to go through this alone."

That night, as Oliver got ready for bed, he felt a bit more at peace. He knew that Worry Wumpus would be there whenever he felt anxious, not to scare him, but to remind him that it was okay to have those feelings.

As he drifted off to sleep, he whispered, "Thank you, Worry Wumpus."

Worry Wumpus, now a comforting presence rather than a source of fear, settled at the foot of the bed, ready to help Oliver face whatever worries came his way.

Chapter 5: Learning to Cope

The morning sun streamed through Oliver's bedroom window as he slowly opened his eyes. To his surprise, Worry Wumpus was still there, sitting at the foot of his bed, looking as concerned as ever.

"Good morning, Oliver," Worry Wumpus said softly. "Today is an important day. we are going to start learning methods to cope with your anxiety."

Oliver sat up, curiosity mixing with his usual nervousness. "Really? How?"

Worry Wumpus smiled gently. "Let us start with something called 'grounding'."

Worry Wumpus explained that many kids feel anxious, especially when they have to do something new or challenging. "It is completely normal," he said. "But there are ways to make it better."

"'Grounding' is a technique to help you feel more connected to the present moment," Worry Wumpus said.

"Look around and name five things you can see, four things you can touch, three things you can hear, two things you can smell, and one thing you can taste. This helps your mind focus on the present moment, instead of your worries."

"Oliver tried 'grounding' and found that it helped him feel calmer. "This is helpful, Worry Wumpus," he said, feeling more at ease.

"I like this! What else can I try?"

Worry Wumpus thought for a moment. "Another useful strategy is to talk about your worries. Sharing your feelings with someone you trust, like your parents or a friend, can make a big difference. They might have ideas that can help, and just knowing you are not alone can be very comforting."

Oliver remembered how talking to his grandma had made him feel better. "That helps. Thanks, Worry Wumpus."

Worry Wumpus smiled. "Remember, Oliver, these are just a couple of the tools you can use. Everyone's different, and it might take some time to find what works best for you. But the important thing is to keep trying and to not give up."

Oliver felt a sense of determination. "I will. And thanks for being here with me."

Worry Wumpus nodded. "You are welcome, Oliver. I am here to remind you that you are stronger than you think. And with these methods, you'll be ready to face whatever comes your way."

That day, as Oliver went about his usual activities, he practiced 'grounding' and deep breathing whenever he felt anxious. He also spent time drawing, reading, and finding comfort in his favorite hobbies. And when he talked to his parents about his worries, he felt a weight lift from his shoulders.

By bedtime, Oliver felt more at ease. He knew that Worry Wumpus would be there to help him through his anxious moments and that with these new methods, he could manage his feelings better.

As he drifted off to sleep, Oliver felt a sense of hope and confidence for the first time in a long while. He was ready to face the challenges ahead, knowing he had the tools and support to help him through.

Chapter 6: The Power of Sharing

Despite using the tricks Worry Wumpus taught him, Oliver still felt anxious. One evening, he decided it was time to talk to his parents about Worry Wumpus and the anxious feelings he had been having. He found them in the kitchen, preparing dinner, and mustered up the courage to tell them everything.

His mom and dad listened carefully. "Oliver, we are so glad you told us," his mom said gently. "It is important to talk about your feelings. We are here to help you."

His dad nodded, placing a reassuring hand on Oliver's shoulder. "Let's come up with a plan together. How about we make a worry box? Whenever you feel anxious, you can write or draw your worry and put it in the box. That way, you can let go of it for a while."

Oliver liked the idea. They found an old shoebox and decorated it with colorful paper and stickers. Oliver wrote down one of his worries and put it inside. He felt a bit lighter.

As they worked on the worry box, Oliver's mom said, "You know, Oliver, it is really important to talk about your feelings. Keeping them inside can make them feel even bigger and scarier. But when you share them, it can help them feel smaller and easier to handle."

Oliver looked up at his mom, feeling a sense of relief. "I didn't want to worry you and Dad."

His dad smiled warmly. "We are your parents, Oliver. It is our job to help you with your worries. We want to know how you are feeling, so we can support you."

They continued decorating the worry box, adding glitter, stickers, and drawings. Oliver wrote down more of his worries, one by one, and placed them inside the box. Each time he did, he felt a little better, as if a weight was being lifted from his shoulders.

"How do you feel now?" his mom asked after they had finished.

"A lot better," Oliver admitted. "It feels good to know you're here to help."

That night, they sat down together and made a plan. They decided that whenever Oliver felt anxious, he could use his 'grounding' method, talk to his parents, or use the worry box. They also agreed to have a family meeting once a week to check in on how everyone was feeling.

"We're a team, Oliver," his dad said. "And teams work together to help each other out."

Oliver felt a warm glow inside. "Thanks Mom and Dad."

Over the next few days, Oliver found that talking to his parents made a big difference. Whenever he felt anxious, he would write down his worries and share them with his mom and dad. They would listen, offer comfort, and help him find ways to feel better.

One evening, as Oliver was putting a worry into the box, he looked at Worry Wumpus, who was sitting nearby. "You know what, Worry Wumpus? Talking to my parents really helps. I don't feel so alone anymore."

Worry Wumpus nodded, his eyes warm and understanding. "I'm glad, Oliver. It's important to have people who care about you and can help you through tough times."

Oliver smiled. "And I have you too."

Worry Wumpus gave a gentle smile. "Yes, Oliver. And together, we'll get through this."

Chapter 7: More Coping Methods

His parents also suggested other ways to cope with anxiety. "You can try imagining a happy place," his mom said. "Close your eyes and imagine a place where you feel safe and happy. Picture every detail and go there in your mind when you feel anxious."

"Exercise is another great way to deal with anxiety," his dad added. "Go for a walk, ride your bike, or play outside. Moving your body helps release the tension."

"And remember," his mom said, "it is okay to say no to Worry Wumpus when you need to. Tell him, 'Thank you for trying to help, but I need some time without you right now.' It is important to set limits with your worries."

That evening, Oliver decided to try to imagine a happy place like his mom had suggested. He closed his eyes and imagined himself at the beach, building sandcastles with his family. He could hear the waves crashing, feel the warm sun on his face, and smell the salty sea air. As he focused on these details, he felt a sense of calm wash over him.

When he opened his eyes, he felt more relaxed. "That helped," he said to himself, making a mental note to use this technique whenever he felt anxious.

The next day, Oliver felt the familiar pangs of anxiety as he thought about school. Remembering his dad's advice, he decided to go for a bike ride. As he pedaled through the neighborhood, the wind in his hair and the rhythmic motion of cycling helped him feel more grounded. The physical activity released some of the tension he had been carrying.

When he returned home, he felt more energized and less anxious. "Exercise really does help," he thought, feeling a sense of accomplishment.

One afternoon, as Oliver was coloring, he felt Worry Wumpus' presence growing stronger. The anxious thoughts started to creep in, making it hard to concentrate. Remembering his mom's words, Oliver took a deep breath and said, "Thank you for trying to help, Worry Wumpus, but I need some time without you right now."

To his surprise, Worry Wumpus nodded and slowly retreated. Oliver felt strong and in control. He realized that he could set limits with his worries and take control of his feelings.

Chapter 8: First Day of School

The first day of third grade arrived. Oliver still felt a little nervous, but he remembered what he had learned. He took deep breaths, thought about his fun summer adventures, and talked to his parents before leaving for school.

When he got to school, he saw his friends and met his new teacher, Mrs. Harper. Everyone seemed friendly and welcoming. Oliver realized that school might not be as scary as he thought. The colorful classroom was filled with posters of animals and a cozy reading corner, making it feel inviting.

However, during the day, Mrs. Harper announced a surprise pop quiz. Oliver felt his heart race and his palms get sweaty. Worry Wumpus appeared next to him with a worried face. But Oliver remembered his coping methods. He took deep breaths, looked around the classroom, and used the 'grounding' method by focusing on the surface of his desk and the sounds of his classmates writing, and thought about his safe place in his treehouse.

Later, in music class, Oliver was asked to sing in front of everyone. He felt a lump in his throat and his legs felt like jelly. Oliver closed his eyes, took a deep breath, and imagined himself in his treehouse, feeling calm and happy.

With his new confidence, Oliver sang his song. He wasn't perfect, but he felt proud of himself for trying. His classmates clapped, and Mrs. Harper gave him a thumbs-up.

As the weeks went by, Oliver faced more challenges. He had to give a presentation in class, deal with a difficult math problem, and participate in a group project. Each time, Worry Wumpus appeared, but Oliver used his coping methods and remembered to set limits. He found that taking deep breaths and imagining his safe place helped him stay calm and focused.

One day, during recess, Oliver noticed his friend, Emma, looking anxious. She was sitting alone on a bench, hugging her knees. Oliver sat next to her and asked, "Are you okay, Emma?"

Emma shook her head. "I feel really nervous about the science project presentation."

Oliver smiled gently. "I know how you feel. I get nervous too. But I have learned some tricks that help. Do you want me to show you?"

Emma nodded. Oliver taught her the deep breathing and 'grounding' methods. They practiced together, and Emma started to feel better. She thanked Oliver and even smiled.

From that day on, Oliver and Emma became close friends, supporting each other through their anxious moments. Oliver felt proud, not only for managing his anxiety, but also for helping others do the same.

Chapter 9: A New Routine

Oliver developed a routine that helped him manage his anxiety. Each morning, he spent a few minutes practicing deep breathing and 'grounding' techniques. He found that these exercises helped him start his day with a sense of calm and focus. He carried a small notebook with him to jot down any worries that popped up during the day. Writing down his thoughts made them feel less overwhelming. He looked forward to putting them in his worry box at home each evening.

In his worry box, Oliver placed the notes he had written throughout the day. This act of physically putting away his worries helped him feel a sense of control over his anxiety. Sometimes, he would go through the notes with his parents, who helped him talk through his feelings and find solutions to his concerns.

He also made sure to spend time doing activities he loved, like playing in his treehouse, drawing, and reading. His treehouse became a special place where he could escape and let his imagination run wild. He decorated it with his favorite posters and even had a little bookshelf where he kept his most beloved books.

Exercise became an important part of his routine too. He and Emma often played soccer or rode their bikes after school. Running around and being active not only made him feel good physically, but also helped clear his mind. On weekends, they would explore the local park, climb trees and pretend they were adventurers on a quest.

In addition to his hobbies, Oliver found comfort in a bedtime routine. Each night, he took a warm bath, read a chapter of his favorite book, and practiced a short meditation before bed. This routine helped him wind down and made sure he got a good night's sleep, which was important for managing his anxiety.

One day, Emma confided in Oliver that she was feeling anxious about an upcoming school play. Remembering how much his routines had helped him, Oliver suggested they practice some of his methods together. They spent their lunch break doing deep breathing exercises. They also talked about their favorite activities to help distract them from their worries. Emma decided to join Oliver in his evening bike rides, finding that the physical activity and fresh air eased her nerves.

As they rode through the neighborhood, they chatted about their day, their dreams, and their fears. These conversations not only brought them closer, but also provided a safe space for them to express their feelings.

Chapter 10: Embracing Worry Wumpus

As time went on, Oliver learned to embrace Worry Wumpus. He understood that Worry Wumpus was not there to harm him, but was a part of him that needed to be managed. He realized it was okay to feel anxious sometimes and that it didn't make him any less brave or strong.

Oliver learned to set limits with Worry Wumpus, only allowing him to visit when necessary. He thanked Worry Wumpus for trying to help, but reminded him that he needed space to be happy and calm.

Oliver's new understanding of Worry Wumpus brought a sense of peace to his life. He no longer felt as though he was battling his anxiety alone. Instead, he saw Worry Wumpus as a part of himself that needed care and attention, just like any other part of his body.

When he felt anxious, he would sit quietly and acknowledge Worry Wumpus, saying, "I know you're here because you care about me, but I need to focus on being calm and happy right now."

This new approach made a big difference in Oliver's daily life. He found it easier to concentrate in school and enjoy his time with friends. One day, his teacher, Mrs. Harper noticed the change in him. "Oliver, you seem more confident lately. What's your secret?"

Oliver smiled and said, "I've learned to understand my Worry Wumpus. Instead of fighting him, I talk to him and set limits. It helps me feel better."

Mrs. Harper nodded approvingly. "That is very wise, Oliver. I am proud of you for finding a way to manage your feelings."

At home, Oliver's parents also noticed the change. During dinner one evening, his dad said, "Oliver, you have been doing so well with your anxiety. We are really proud of you. What has been helping you?

Oliver explained how he had started talking to Worry Wumpus and setting limits. His parents listened intently, impressed by his new change. "That's a wonderful strategy, Oliver," his mom said. "We are so glad you are finding ways to feel better."

As Oliver continued to practice his coping methods, he became more skilled at recognizing when Worry Wumpus was about to visit. He would take a deep breath and remind himself of all the methods he had learned. Whether it was deep breathing, 'grounding', or imagining his safe place; Oliver knew he had the tools to manage his anxiety.

Conclusion

Oliver still had moments of anxiety, but he knew how to handle them. Worry Wumpus visited less often and only when truly needed, reminding Oliver of the coping methods they had learned together. Each visit became a gentle reminder that it was okay to feel anxious sometimes and that it did not make him who he was.

Oliver felt proud of himself for facing his fears and knew that with time, he would feel even better. He also found joy in helping others, like Emma, who faced similar struggles. They often teamed up for school projects and even started a small support group at school, where they shared their experiences and taught other kids about coping methods. The group became a source of comfort and strength for many students, and Oliver felt proud to be making a difference.

At home, Oliver's family celebrated his progress. They often spent evenings talking about their day and sharing stories, creating a safe space where Oliver felt understood and supported. Family game nights and movie marathons became regular events, filled with laughter and joy.

Oliver's confidence continued to grow. He took on new challenges, like joining the school band and participating in activities in town. Each experience taught him more about himself and his ability to overcome his worries. He learned to see Worry Wumpus as a companion on his journey, not an enemy.

In the end, Oliver's life was filled with moments of joy, connection, and growth. He faced each day with a sense of purpose and a heart full of gratitude. He knew that he could handle whatever challenges came his way, and he looked forward to a bright and hopeful future.

Oliver's story shows how strong and brave people can be when they do not give up. It reminds us all that, no matter what we face, we can rise above and create a life filled with love, courage, and endless possibilities.

Author's Note

Dear Parents and Caregivers,

"Oliver and the Anxiety Monster" is designed to help children understand and cope with anxiety. As a parent or caregiver, it is important to recognize the signs of anxiety in your child and provide them with the support they need. Here are some additional methods and resources to help you and your child manage anxiety effectively:

1. Open Communication:
- Encourage your child to talk about their feelings.
- Create a safe and non-judgmental space for them to express their worries and fears.
- Validate their feelings by acknowledging their anxiety and letting them know it is okay to feel this way.

2. Establish Routines:
- Consistent daily routines can provide a sense of stability and predictability, helping to reduce anxiety.
- Include calming activities, such as reading, drawing, or listening to music as part of their daily routine.

3. Mindfulness and Relaxation Techniques:

- Teach your child mindfulness exercises, such as deep breathing, progressive muscle relaxation, or guided imagery to help them stay calm.
- Practice these techniques together to show your support and reinforce their effectiveness.

4. Encourage Physical Activity:

- Regular physical activity can help reduce anxiety and improve overall well-being.
- Encourage your child to participate in activities they enjoy, such as playing outside, biking, or swimming.

5. Create a Worry Box:

- Make a worry box where your child can write down their worries and place them in the box. This can help them externalize their anxieties and feel a sense of relief.

6. Limit Exposure to Stressors:

- Monitor and limit exposure to stressful situations or stimuli, such as certain media content or over-scheduling activities.
- Create a calm and relaxing environment at home to promote a sense of security.

7. Professional Help:

- If your child's anxiety persists or worsens, consider seeking professional help from a therapist or counselor who specializes in children's mental health.
- Many schools offer counseling services, and your child's pediatrician can provide referrals to mental health professionals.

8. Support Groups and Resources:

- Join support groups for parents of children with anxiety to share experiences, gain insights, and receive support.
- Utilize resources from reputable organizations, such as the Anxiety and Depression Association of America (ADAA), the National Institute of Mental Health (NIMH), and local mental health services.

9. Educational Materials:

- Read books and watch videos about anxiety with your child to help them understand their feelings and learn coping methods.
- Use age-appropriate materials to educate your child about anxiety and the importance of mental health.

Remember, you are not alone in this journey. With the right support and methods, you can help your child manage their anxiety and thrive. Together, we can make a positive difference in their lives.